Fr. Jay T Magpuyo, ordained on December 8, 2017, is serving in the Diocese of East Anglia, in a spirit of Faith and community. His pastoral journey led him to various parishes. Currently, he is the Parish Priest of Sacred Heart and St. Margaret Mary Catholic Church in Dereham, Norfolk, a quaint parish where communal relationships are nourished in Christ.

Fr Jay T Magpuyo

METHOD PRAYER

AUSTIN MACAULEY PUBLISHERS™

LONDON • CAMBRIDGE • NEW YORK • SHARJAH

A CIP catalogue record for this title is available from the British Library.

ISBN 9781035861323 (Paperback)
ISBN 9781035861330 (ePub e-book)

www.austinmacauley.com

First Published 2024
Austin Macauley Publishers Ltd®
1 Canada Square
Canary Wharf
London
E14 5AA

Introduction

The power of prayer has been celebrated and revered across generations and civilizations, remaining an unyielding cornerstone of human spirituality. In the shifting sands of time, amidst rapid technological progress and cultural evolution, this ancient practice has remained a stalwart refuge for those seeking spiritual sustenance. A practice that has been both a silent whisper of solitary souls and the collective voice of congregations, prayer is a universal testament to humanity's innate yearning to reach out to the Divine.

Today's hyper-connected world, where technology governs our every moment, and where information floods our senses at an unprecedented rate, poses a unique challenge. The cacophony of modern life often drowns the innermost whispers of our spirit, creating a chasm between our everyday experiences and our deeper spiritual desires. It is against this backdrop that the "Method Prayer" shines as a beacon of hope, a gentle reminder of the timeless power of heartfelt communion with the Divine.

This book promises to be more than just an exposition of words. It seeks to be a spiritual guide, a roadmap to the very core of our being. Using the Method Prayer as a guidepost, the reader is invited to journey into the uncharted depths of the soul, where raw emotion meets profound faith. Like the explorers of yesteryears who embarked on quests to discover new lands, the reader is encouraged to navigate the intricate labyrinth of their heart and spirit.

The Christian tradition, with its rich tapestry of beliefs, rituals, and practices, serves as the backdrop for this exploration. The Method Prayer, deeply rooted in this tradition, offers a structured approach to prayer. It emphasizes not just the words we utter, but the intent, the emotion, and the profound faith behind them. It challenges the believer to move beyond rote recitation and to engage in a profound, heartfelt dialogue with the Almighty.

At its core, prayer is an intimate conversation, a sacred dance of the soul with the Divine. But Method Prayer goes a step further. It encourages a methodical, intentional approach to this sacred act. It prompts the believer to delve deep, to introspect, and to connect with God on a level that transcends the mundane. The book doesn't just prescribe a formula; it ignites a passion, kindling the flames of faith and spirituality.

In the relentless hustle of modern life, where moments of silence are rare and sacred spaces often invaded by the digital realm, the Method Prayer emerges as a sanctuary. It offers a respite, a sacred space where the soul can rejuvenate, reflect, and reconnect with its Creator. It underscores the idea that even in this age of instant gratification and digital dominance, the ancient art of prayer retains its unparalleled power to heal, guide, and transform.

As you leaf through the chapters of this enlightening guide, it is our hope that you find more than just teachings and methodologies. May you find a mirror reflecting your deepest desires, fears, and hopes. May it inspire introspection, ignite passion, and instil a deeper appreciation for the profound act of prayer. Let this journey not just be about understanding a method but about rediscovering the ageless bond between humanity and the Divine.

Method Prayer is not just a testament to the transformative power of prayer but also a tribute to humanity's timeless quest for spiritual enlightenment. As you embark on this soulful journey, may you be reminded of the boundless potential that lies within, waiting to be tapped. In the sacred act of prayer, you hold the key to unlocking a world of spiritual abundance, deeper understanding, and unparalleled connection with the Divine. Let this be your compass, guiding you towards a richer, more fulfilling spiritual experience.

Chapter 1
Prayer in Christian Traditions: A Timeless Journey of Faith and Devotion

Amid the ever-changing mosaic of human spirituality, one practice remains a cornerstone: Christian prayer. A practice that not only transcends the boundaries of time but also intertwines the lives of modern-day believers with the fervent spirits of those from centuries past. Prayer is not just a ritual; it's a profound journey, an exploration deep into the very essence of Christian spirituality, and a testament to the relentless quest for divine communion.

This spiritual odyssey takes its roots from the ancient streets of Jerusalem. This city, with its pulsating spiritual energy, seems to breathe with the weight of myriad prayers whispered over millennia. Its ancient walls and narrow alleys echo with the passionate invocations of prophets and psalmists. Jerusalem stands as a spiritual lodestar, guiding generations in their quest for divine connection.

It's within the embrace of this city that the seeds of Christian prayer were first sown, rooted deeply in the traditions of the Old Testament. The foundations lie in the sacred words of the Old Testament, a text that crystallizes the earliest yearnings for divine communion. The Psalms, with their poignant verses of praise, lament, and hope, form the heart of this legacy. These verses are not just poetic renditions; they represent the raw, unfiltered emotions of individuals reaching out to the Divine, setting the tone for Christian prayers for centuries to come.

As time unfurled, the emergence of the early Christian church marked a pivotal chapter in the evolution of prayer. The church wasn't just a place of worship; it was a sanctuary for believers during times of intense persecution. Prayer, within these sacred halls, was more than just a ritual; it was an act of defiance, perseverance, and unity. It became the lifeblood of these early communities, binding them together with threads of shared faith and hope.

Central to this narrative is the Lord's Prayer. Handed down by Jesus to his disciples, this prayer encapsulates the essence of Christian devotion. It is a mosaic of reverence, hope, and submission, each word resonating with profound wisdom. This isn't just a prayer; it's a guiding philosophy, a beacon that has illuminated the path for believers across different denominations and traditions. Its timeless nature is a testament to its universal appeal, holding a mirror to the core tenets of Christianity.

However, the story of Christian prayer is not just an artefact of history. It is a living, breathing tradition that continues to evolve, adapting to the rhythms of contemporary life. Modern expressions of Christian prayer are a testament to its enduring relevance. Today's believers, much like their ancestors, find solace in the embrace of prayer, whether it's within the magnificent confines of age-old cathedrals or the intimate corners of their homes. From the structured liturgies echoing in high churches to the spontaneous, impassioned pleas of individuals, the spirit of prayer remains unaltered. It's a testament to the universal need for hope, strength, and a deeper connection with the Divine.

The journey of Christian prayer reflects the broader quest for spiritual fulfilment. It charts the evolution of human yearning, from the ancient streets of Jerusalem to the bustling avenues of modern cities. It's a reminder that regardless of the era or context, the human spirit invariably seeks out the Divine. Prayer, in the Christian tradition, is more than just a practice; it's a legacy, a timeless bridge connecting generations of believers in their shared quest for divine communion.

A Timeless Journey into the Soul of Christian Tradition

We carry with us the profound realization that Christian prayer is not a relic of the past but a living, breathing entity that continues to evolve. It offers solace to the weary, hope to the despondent, and a bridge to the Divine for those who dare to cross it. This chapter is not merely an academic endeavour; it is an enthralling journey through time, an odyssey into the very soul of Christian tradition. It reminds us that, through the threads of history, faith endures, and prayer remains an enduring expression of the human spirit's longing for the Divine.

The Book of Psalms, nestled within the ancient texts of the Old Testament, is often heralded as the cornerstone of Christian prayer. It is here, in this collection of poignant songs and hymns, where the deep roots of Christian worship first took hold. With its vast array of human emotions, from the heights of joy to the depths of despair, the Psalms encompass the full human experience in the divine presence. This emotional tapestry not only reflects our complex relationship with God but also shapes the very nature of worship and spiritual dialogue that Christians engage in even today.

These 150 Psalms provide a language for the inexpressible aspects of our journey with God. The psalmists, with their unguarded expressions of faith, fear, love, and longing, extend an invitation to the faithful to approach God with a similar candour. They model a prayer life that is not limited to moments of peace and certainty but also encompasses times of turmoil and questioning. This diversity in the Psalms assures the believer that every human emotion can be brought before the Creator.

Joy is often a prominent theme, where the Psalmist sings of God's unfailing love and faithfulness, while despair and lament highlight the struggles and pains of life, urging the worshiper to cling to God's promise of deliverance. Hope is interwoven through the verses, a steadfast anchor in the stormy seas of doubt and fear, while repentance brings about a heartfelt turning back to God, acknowledging one's shortcomings and the merciful nature of the divine.

The raw vulnerability evident in the Psalms sets a profound standard for the honesty and depth that characterizes Christian prayer. The psalmists bear their souls, revealing a spiritual openness that has defined the way believers communicate with God for generations. The candour in these ancient songs demonstrates a relationship with the Divine that is not hindered by pretence but is open, sincere, and deeply personal.

Throughout the centuries, the Psalms have been woven into the fabric of Christian liturgy. Their words resonate in the echoes of church halls, their themes and phrases integrated into the hymns sung by congregations across the world. The Psalms also provide a framework for personal devotion, as believers find solace, encouragement, and guidance in their timeless verses. Whether chanted in a corporate setting or whispered in a quiet room, the Psalms serve as a bridge connecting the individual soul to the divine presence.

The influence of the Psalms on Christian worship and devotion cannot be overstated. As much as they are prayers, they are also teachings — a school of prayer that educates the believer in the art of communion with God. The emotional honesty of the Psalms gives permission to lay bare our fears, voice our doubts, and admit our weaknesses, while also emboldening us to proclaim our hopes and affirm our faith.

The Psalms stand as a profound legacy in Christian prayer, demonstrating that an authentic prayer life embraces the full spectrum of human emotions. They encourage a boldness in prayer, to approach the throne of grace with the same raw emotion that the psalmists did, reflecting the real conditions of the human heart. The Psalms teach that prayer is not about the right words but about the right heart — one that seeks God in truth.

Continuing to echo through time, the Psalms guide believers on a path of spiritual connection and transformation. They serve as an enduring testament to the enduring power of prayer — a power that captures the heart's deepest cries and the soul's loftiest praises. They remind us that prayer, in its essence, is about presence — being present with God as our full, authentic selves, just as the psalmists were. And so, as they have for thousands of years, the Psalms remain a compass for the Christian soul, guiding it through the ever-changing landscape of life and into the embrace of the divine.

The Early Christian Church – Communal Prayer and Perseverance

In the intricate tapestry of Christian prayer, the communal nature of the early Christian church stands out prominently. This nascent community, emerging amidst a myriad of social, political, and religious complexities, leaned heavily on prayer as its unifying backbone. Born in an era of persecution, when believers often found themselves marginalized, the very act of communal prayer became both a refuge and a form of silent resistance.

The catacombs of Rome – subterranean burial sites – bear silent witness to this clandestine faith. Within these dimly lit, winding passages, early Christians sought a safe haven from the outside world's threats. In the shadows beneath a bustling city, they discovered a profound sense of community and solace. Here, prayer was more than just a ritual; it was a lifeline. These underground gatherings underscored their unwavering commitment to their beliefs and each other. It emphasized the depth of their faith, which thrived even in the face of external threats.

This period of persecution gave birth to a form of prayer that was profoundly unifying. As they came together in the heart of the catacombs, the act of worship became a shared response to their shared challenges. The adversity they faced was countered by their collective resilience, fuelled by prayer. Through their combined supplications, they drew strength, courage, and a reinforced sense of belonging. The Christian community, in these formative years, was being shaped and defined by the very adversities it faced.

As the church's structure began to evolve, so did its approach to prayer. The early Christian liturgies emerged, offering a more structured form of worship. These included hymns, scripture readings, and communal recitations. The liturgy was more than just a set of rituals; it deepened the spiritual experiences of its participants. It provided a framework, a shared language of devotion that resonated with the assembled faithful. This framework, in many ways, solidified the communal nature of early Christian prayer, emphasizing unity even as diverse forms of worship began to emerge.

The perseverance of the early Christian community is, in many ways, a reflection of its commitment to prayer. Despite facing constant threats and challenges, this community grew, thrived, and left an indelible mark on the Christian tradition. The echoes of their collective voices, raised in prayer from the depths of the catacombs, continue to resonate today. Their unwavering faith, and the communal nature of their prayer, serve as a reminder of the power of unity, resilience, and shared purpose.

Today, as we journey through Christian history, the story of the early Christian church stands as a beacon. It is a testament to the enduring power of faith and the role of communal prayer in forging connections. It reminds us that even in the darkest times, when believers might feel isolated or threatened, coming together in prayer can light the way, offering solace, strength, and unity. The early Christian church's legacy is one of unwavering commitment to shared devotion, a beacon of unity in the face of adversity, and a reminder of the transformative power of communal prayer.

The Timeless Relevance of the Lord's Prayer

Diving deep into the core of Christian prayer, we are met with the enduring legacy of the Lord's Prayer—a sacred touchstone that bridges the past, present, and future of Christian spirituality. This venerable orison, also revered as the "Our Father" or "Pater Noster," is more than just a liturgical recitation; it is a profound encapsulation of the Christian relationship with the Divine.

Attributed directly to Jesus, the Lord's Prayer is a divine gift, a treasure of wisdom shared with His disciples. This cherished prayer serves not merely as an invocation but also as a guide on how believers should resonate with God, envisioning Him as a nurturing and caring Father. Each word, each phrase of this prayer, is laden with profound significance. Beginning with "Our Father", it lays the foundation for an intimate relationship with God, emphasizing His omnipresence and benevolence. The ensuing phrases, such as "Thy kingdom come, Thy will be done", illustrate a roadmap to devotion, reflecting aspirations for both personal spiritual growth and global harmony.

The prayer's universality is undeniably one of its most outstanding facets. It binds Christians of various denominations and traditions, forming an indomitable link of shared faith across the globe. This simplicity, coupled with its deep spiritual resonance, makes it a prayer for all – an invocation that is inclusive and welcoming. Recited with fervour by millions, the Lord's Prayer fosters a collective spiritual consciousness, reinforcing a sense of unity and shared purpose among believers.

Delving into its historical context, the prayer's omnipresence in the Gospels and its preservation through oral traditions and scriptures played an instrumental role in early Christian prayer practices. As we trace its historical trajectory, we discern its adaptation and pivotal role in the evolution of early Christianity. While it is rooted in ancient wisdom, its contemporary relevance is undeniable. Today's world, rife with complexities, seeks solace in this prayer, drawing from its timeless teachings. Theologians, scholars, and spiritual visionaries over the ages have offered diverse interpretations, each unravelling a layer of its depth, making it an enduring beacon of guidance in today's fast-paced world.

The Lord's Prayer transcends its textual confines, serving as a wellspring for profound spiritual contemplation. Each recitation is an introspective journey, urging individuals to delve deeper into their spiritual selves. It teaches surrender to God's will, evokes gratitude for His daily blessings, and emphasizes the significance of forgiveness and reconciliation. Far from being a mere ritualistic chant, it is a transformative experience, a call to self-examination, fostering a bond with the Divine.

In essence, the Lord's Prayer is not just a prayer; it is a spiritual compass, guiding believers across generations. Its timeless themes offer a sanctuary of reflection, nurturing souls and shaping the ethos of Christian living. As it continues to be a cornerstone of Christian devotion, it stands as a testament to the undying power of faith and the eternal journey of spiritual exploration. Through this prayer, believers are reminded of their divine purpose, inspiring them to lead lives that resonate with its profound teachings. In its words, we find solace, guidance, and an ever-present connection to the Divine.

Chapter 2
The Symphony of Christian Prayer

Christian prayer, much like a symphony, is a harmonious blend of diverse melodies, each resonating with distinct emotions and spiritual purposes. This celestial symphony is not just a mere formality or ritual, but a rich tapestry of heartfelt conversations between the believer and the Divine. Drawing parallels between the multifaceted nature of a symphony and Christian prayer helps illuminate the profound depth and range of spiritual communication.

A symphony, with its intricate layers of music, evokes a spectrum of emotions, transporting the listener on a journey from tranquil contemplation to peaks of exuberance. Similarly, Christian prayer isn't a monolithic practice but a dynamic interplay of various forms, each serving a unique spiritual need. Just as every instrument in a symphony has its role, so does each type of Christian prayer contribute to the believer's spiritual chorus.

Among these prayer types, adoration stands out as a joyful exaltation, praising God's boundless majesty, much like the crescendo in a musical piece. It's an awe-inspired recognition of God's grandeur, setting the tone for the spiritual journey. Following this, confession acts as a soulful melody, allowing believers to acknowledge their shortcomings, and seek divine forgiveness and grace, akin to a gentle, cleansing rain.

Thanksgiving is another vibrant refrain, where gratitude is expressed for life's myriad blessings. This jubilant appreciation is akin to the celebratory moments in a symphony, where joy and contentment take centre stage. On the other hand, supplication and intercession are more intimate, resembling a poignant duet. Here, the believer presents personal needs and the concerns of others, weaving a heartfelt narrative of hope and compassion.

Petition, a personal and direct dialogue with God, mirrors the quiet, introspective moments in music, where one seeks guidance and clarity. Meditation, the contemplative strand in this tapestry, allows believers to immerse themselves in sacred texts, drawing parallels to a serene sonata, fostering deeper understanding and connection.

In essence, Christian prayer, with its diverse types, forms a spiritual symphony. This symphony is a testament to the multifaceted nature of human experiences and emotions in their relationship with the Divine. Each prayer, like every note in a musical piece, holds significance, contributing to a harmonious and enriching spiritual journey. Through this symphonic metaphor, we come to appreciate the depth, range, and beauty of Christian prayer, an eternal melody that connects the soul to the Divine.

Adoration: The Grand Overture of the Soul

The spiritual journey of a Christian is replete with moments of reflection, reverence, and communion with the Divine. Of these, adoration stands distinct, akin to the grand overture in a symphonic masterpiece. It is the preamble to the deeper engagements of the soul, setting the tone for the spiritual saga that unfolds. This beautiful act of adoration, deep-seated in its reverence for the divine, can be visualized as a sacred dance within a magnificent cathedral, an emblem of the soul's inner sanctuary.

As one steps into this metaphorical cathedral of adoration, the senses are enveloped in a divine ambience. The soft luminescence of countless candles bathes the sanctuary in a golden glow, casting mesmerizing patterns on the ancient walls and vaulted ceilings. These shifting silhouettes, paired with the ethereal fragrance of burning incense, transport the believer to a realm beyond the mundane. It is as if the very air is imbued with spirituality, each breath drawing the soul closer to the Divine.

In this hallowed space, individual worshippers converge, adding their unique essence to the collective symphony of devotion. The combined energy of numerous souls in reverence creates an atmosphere that resonates with palpable spirituality. Intermittent murmurs of prayers and the melodic strains of hymns punctuate the profound silence, reflecting the depth of awe and adoration shared by all.

At the heart of this adoration lies an overwhelming recognition of the divine's majesty and splendour. The soul, humbled by the sheer vastness and beauty of the Creator, basks in a state of surrender. In this profound moment of realization, words take on a sacred significance. Prayers, hymns, and chants, expressed with deep fervour, become the soul's offerings at the altar of the divine. These aren't mere recitations; they are the deepest yearnings of a heart captivated by the divine's presence.

Music, the universal language of emotions, weaves its magic into this tapestry of adoration. The cathedral's confines echo with harmonious melodies, a blend of ancient chants and contemporary hymns. This music, much like a gentle river, flows seamlessly, bridging the gap between the terrestrial and the celestial, guiding the soul on its journey towards the divine.

Yet, even as words and melodies fill the cathedral, there are intervals of profound, contemplative silence. These moments, devoid of any verbal or sonic expression, are rich in spiritual communication. Here, in the quietude, the soul dialogues with the Divine in a language that transcends words – a silent communion, a mystical exchange.

The act of adoration seems to suspend the relentless march of time. The cacophony of everyday life fades, replaced by a serene stillness where the soul and the divine converge. In this divine dance of reverence, worshippers find themselves enveloped by an overwhelming sense of God's omnipresence, moved by His boundless grace and glory.

This inaugural movement of the soul's symphony serves as a poignant reminder of the privilege and profoundness of standing in the divine's presence. It rejuvenates the spiritual essence, reigniting the flame of faith and deepening the ethereal bond. In essence, adoration, as the grand overture, encapsulates the soul's boundless capacity for reverence, setting the stage for the deeper spiritual engagements that follow. Through adoration, believers not only acknowledge the awe-striking nature of the divine but also celebrate the human spirit's innate ability to connect, worship, and revel in the glory of God.

Confession: The Soul's Path to Redemption

Christian prayer comprises various movements, and among these, confession emerges as the soul's cleansing aria. It is a profound act, resonating deeply within the human psyche, mirroring the innate longing for absolution, healing, and redemption. The evocative imagery of an individual, isolated and vulnerable, kneeling in a dim, tranquil confessional booth, serves as a powerful metaphor for the soul's journey to redemption.

In this hallowed space, the ambience is one of silence and reflection. Soft luminescence provides just enough light to cast gentle shadows, enveloping the penitent in an atmosphere of introspection and intimacy. The confessional, by its very design, is meant to be a place of solitude – a space where one faces not just God, but oneself. Here, the individual takes on the role of the penitent, humbling oneself in a display of pure vulnerability.

To understand confession is to grasp the human need for acknowledgement of one's fallibility. It's a moment of stark honesty, where the soul acknowledges its sins, its missteps, and its frailties. In this intimate dialogue with the Divine, the penitent seeks understanding and compassion, recognizing that it is only through God's mercy that true forgiveness can be attained. The confessional becomes the arena where judgment is set aside, and replaced by boundless compassion.

Often, the act of confessing can be likened to a soulful aria – a melody that exudes pain, remorse, but ultimately, hope. The words spoken in sincerity by the penitent become the poignant notes of this melody, each articulation symbolizing a step towards reconciliation and healing. This cleansing process, like clear waters washing away impurities, serves to rejuvenate the spirit, offering it a fresh start.

The essence of confession is vulnerability. Within the confines of the confessional, one is laid bare, revealing struggles, doubts, and sins. Such an act necessitates profound trust – a belief that in revealing one's deepest vulnerabilities, they will be met with divine love and acceptance. In this sacred interaction, solace is found, offering respite to the beleaguered soul.

Yet, confession extends beyond the mere acknowledgement of sins. It's a heartfelt request for redemption – a recognition of one's own dependence on divine mercy. Through this act, the soul reaches out, seeking God's embrace and understanding that His grace is the road to spiritual renewal.

Confession's transformative power cannot be understated. This cleansing aria of the soul serves as a reminder of the human condition – we err, we falter, yet we yearn for redemption. By laying bare one's imperfections before the divine, there's a purification process, leading the soul towards renewal and closer to God.

The act of confession, the soul's cleansing aria, is a beacon of hope. It signifies the lifting of the weight of guilt and the reestablishment of a bond with God. Confession stands testament to the belief in divine mercy – that every sin, no matter how grave, can find forgiveness, and every soul, no matter how lost, can find its path to redemption.

Thanksgiving: Harmony of Gratitude

In the grand composition of Christian devotion, thanksgiving rings out as a jubilant refrain. It's the soul's harmonious response to life's bounty – a heartfelt celebration of gratitude that binds us together in moments of collective joy and recognition of divine generosity. As a quintessential expression of the prayerful life, thanksgiving is an act that elevates the mundane, sanctifying our daily bread and the air we breathe into the sacraments of the Almighty's ongoing creation.

Envision the scene of this spiritual concert: a table lavishly set, brimming with the earth's offerings. The air is thick with the mingling scents of roasted harvests and sweet pies, evoking an ambience of comfort and providence. Family and friends encircle this table, a fellowship of diverse faces alight with the glow of candles and connection. Their laughter and shared tales are the melody to which hearts dance in gratitude, reflecting the depth and variety of life's bestowed riches.

This thanksgiving is an ensemble piece, a chorus that swells to acknowledge the multitude of blessings that texture our existence. Each note sung is a word of thanks, each harmony a recognition of life's beauty and complexity. It's the point in the symphony where the soul revels in the acknowledgement of good that spills forth in abundance, whether in health, in the steadfast love of companions, in the splendour of creation, or the simple joys that embroider our days with happiness.

Beyond mere liturgy, this movement of thanksgiving is the soul's expression of an ever-present truth: that we are cradled by a divine providence. It invites us to a moment of introspection, to consider the facets of life that kindle thankfulness – a loving gesture, a moment of quietude in nature, the sheer miracle of existence. In this reflection, we find our spirits lifted, our hearts expanded to receive and reciprocate this universal grace.

This act of giving thanks binds us not only to the Creator but to one another, weaving a tapestry of communal recognition. As we lift our voices in gratitude, we acknowledge that every breath, every morsel, every beat of the heart is a gift. Such acknowledgement is not passive; it's an active, potent force that cements our place in a world teeming with God's love and mercy.

Thanksgiving, then, is more than a mere pause in prayer – it's a state of being. In cultivating a grateful heart, we shift our gaze from scarcity to abundance, from wanting to acknowledging. This transformation is not just personal; it echoes throughout the community, uplifting others and magnifying the symphony of collective gratitude.

As we contribute our voices to this chorus of thanks, we do more than express our individual joy; we join a celestial harmony that celebrates the continuous and loving act of creation itself. In thanksgiving, every soul is both soloist and part of the choir, singing a melody of appreciation that resonates through the vaults of heaven and across the breadth of the earth.

Supplication and Intercession: Echoes of Devotion

In the multifaceted realm of Christian devotion, the tandem of supplication and intercession shines as a profound duet, echoing the core aspirations and desires of humanity. This duet, a genuine dialogue with the divine, encapsulates the essence of human longing and altruistic love, as it dances through the vast soundscape of heartfelt prayer.

Picture a scene set in tranquillity and reverence. Two individuals, perhaps close friends or spiritual companions, stand together in solemnity. Their demeanour, one of submission and humility, reflects the gravity of their communion with God. The serene ambience they create isn't just a physical one; it's a deep spiritual connection, resonating with hope, trust, and unwavering faith.

The melody of supplication, the first part of this duet, is one of personal yearning and humble petition. Here, the individual unveils their innermost desires, aspirations, and anxieties. With every rise and fall of their prayer, they open up to God, revealing their most profound vulnerabilities, dreams, and fears. It's a moment of raw authenticity, where the barriers between the soul and the divine crumble, forging a bond of trust and intimacy. Supplication, in its essence, is the soul's candid conversation with its Creator, seeking guidance, solace, and affirmation.

The harmonious counterpart, intercession, is the prayer of selfless advocacy. This is where the individual extends their heart's cry beyond personal needs, enveloping the concerns of others. Through intercession, these friends become messengers of God's compassion and mercy, pleading on behalf of others. It reflects a deep-seated Christian conviction: the belief in the interconnected tapestry of human lives. In this act, the individual showcases selflessness, placing the well-being and needs of others before their own, championing the causes of those in distress, and becoming beacons of hope.

This symphonic duet of supplication and intercession reverberates with the very core of human experience. At its heart, it is a longing for divine connection, understanding, and compassion. It's a reflection of the Christian ethos of love, where personal communication with God evolves into a broader expression of love for humanity. Through these prayers, one not only seeks personal solace but also endeavours to become a vessel of God's grace for others.

In sum, the heartfelt duet of supplication and intercession within the Christian prayer narrative serves as a poignant reminder of the transformative essence of prayer. It is not just a monologue directed at the heavens but a bidirectional exchange that shapes our spirit and guides our actions. It's a call to recognize our personal vulnerabilities, find comfort in the divine embrace, and in turn, extend that very embrace to envelop those around us in love and compassion.

Petition: The Soul's Serenade to the Divine

Amid the vast ensemble of Christian prayer, the tender movement of petition stands out with poignant distinction. Think of it as a soul's personal serenade – an intimate ballad, softly sung to the heavens, seeking a connection that transcends the earthly realm. Picture, if you will, an individual – alone yet not isolated, nestled within the serene embrace of a verdant garden. In this secluded haven, the soft murmurs of a heartfelt dialogue with the Creator unfold, enveloped by nature's gentle symphony.

Such gardens, teeming with life and echoing with the whispers of the breeze, serve as sanctuaries for the spirit.

Here, away from the world's cacophony, the atmosphere brims with a tranquillity that magnifies the soul's yearnings. Birds provide a gentle accompaniment, flowers lend their fragrance, and trees stand as silent witnesses to this vulnerable exchange, amplifying the sincerity of the moment.

The act of petition is both delicate and profound. This form of prayer is not about grand gestures or elaborate rituals but centres on raw, unfiltered vulnerability. With earnestness and simplicity, the petitioner reaches out to the divine, seeking understanding, guidance, and grace. Every word, every pause, is an invitation for divine insight, a plea for comfort in moments of despair, and a quest for light amidst the shadows.

This prayer, this personal serenade, is rooted in authenticity. Unlike recited verses or rehearsed chants, it emerges spontaneously from the soul's deepest chambers. Every note resonates with genuine emotion – a fusion of hope, desperation, love, and sometimes even doubt. It is this honesty, this unvarnished truth, that renders the petition so powerful and resonant.

Such moments of communion underscore the essence of the human experience. They acknowledge our vulnerabilities, our moments of frailty, and the inevitable uncertainties that mark our journey. But more importantly, they highlight our innate need to connect, to reach out and find solace in a higher presence. Through these personal serenades, we are reminded that even in our weakest moments, we are never truly alone. For in the silent spaces between our words, in the pauses between our pleas, the divine listens, understands, and responds, turning our solitary song into a harmonious duet of hope and healing.

Meditation: The Soul's Journey through the Contemplative Sonata

Within the expansive landscape of Christian prayer, the act of meditation emerges as a distinct movement, akin to a contemplative sonata. This deep-seated form of spiritual engagement offers individuals a structured path to introspection, guiding them toward a more profound connection with the divine. Picture a centuries-old monastery, nestled amidst rolling hills. Within its thick stone walls, monks find solace, immersing themselves in meditative practices, their hearts echoing with the rhythms of sacred texts.

Such monasteries have long stood as beacons of spiritual refuge. The very atmosphere within these sanctuaries seems to hum with an otherworldly stillness, providing a fitting backdrop for a soul's deep dive into meditation. Amidst this tranquillity, monks and practitioners alike dedicate hours, sometimes days, to the contemplation of holy scriptures, fostering a deep bond between their spirit and the divine word.

Structured like a musical sonata, meditation within the Christian tradition is marked by carefully orchestrated phases. Starting with a gentle invitation into God's presence, practitioners slowly immerse themselves in sacred readings, letting the words wash over them. Much like how a sonata unfolds in distinct movements, each with its rhythm and mood, meditative prayer guides the soul through layers of reflection, self-examination, and spiritual communion.

In this meditative sonata, scriptures are not merely read; they are experienced. Every passage, every verse, becomes a living entity, speaking directly to the practitioner's heart. This process is deeply intentional, allowing ample time for the words to seep into the soul, illuminating and transforming from within. The slow, deliberate pace is its strength, ensuring that the transformative essence of each scripture is fully absorbed.

This rich tapestry of Christian prayer, with its diverse movements of adoration, confession, gratitude, petition, and, of course, meditation, creates a harmonious symphony of spiritual expression. Each facet of prayer adds depth and nuance to this divine orchestra, articulating the myriad emotions, longings, and revelations of the human spirit.

At the heart of this spiritual concert lies the contemplative sonata of meditation. As one delves deeper into this practice, it becomes clear that it is more than just a passive act of reading. It's an active engagement, a dance of the soul with the divine, set to the timeless melodies of sacred texts. It beckons us to pause, reflect, and be reborn through the ancient wisdom contained within these scriptures, drawing us ever closer to the eternal embrace of the divine.

Chapter 3
Understanding Method Prayer: Unveiling the Art of Soulful Communion

Method Prayer invites us into a realm where prayer transcends the ordinary and becomes a masterpiece of divine communion. This chapter delves into the metaphor of an artist's canvas, where the strokes of intention, the colours of emotion, and the intricacies of connection meld together to create a profound and transformative experience.

Picture the canvas of Method Prayer as an empty space, waiting to be adorned with the brushstrokes of intentionality and the vibrant hues of emotion. Each prayer is a deliberate stroke, each word a hue, and each moment of stillness a pause to reflect on the canvas. In this sacred space, we set our spiritual intention, merging our heart's desires with divine guidance, much like an artist skilfully crafting their work of art.

Emotions, like a vivid palette of colours, infuse life into our spiritual canvas. We dip our brush into the wells of joy, sorrow, love, and awe, allowing our emotions to flow onto the canvas of our prayers. Just as colours add depth and dimension to a painting, emotions enrich and authenticate our communion with the divine in Method Prayer.

Connection is the tapestry that weaves Method Prayer into our daily lives. Like an artist who frames their artwork, we frame the sacred within the mundane. Every moment becomes an opportunity for prayer, from washing dishes to taking a walk, as we extend the canvas of Method Prayer beyond the confines of sacred spaces.

The Art of Intentionality: Crafting a Spiritual Masterpiece

In the vast mosaic of spiritual practices, Method Prayer stands out as a beacon of purposeful engagement. Central to this practice is the principle of intentionality – a deliberate and conscious approach to shaping one's spiritual journey. This principle elevates prayer from a mere act of ritual to an art form, where every utterance, thought, and pause becomes an intricate brushstroke on the vast canvas of the soul. Like a master artist, intentionality empowers the practitioner to paint a vivid portrait of their spiritual aspirations, merging the profound depths of personal yearning with the boundless realm of divine connection.

Picture a tranquil studio, where an artist stands before an untouched canvas. The air is thick with anticipation. Each choice – whether it's the selection of a colour or the sweep of a brush – will imprint a piece of the artist's soul onto the canvas. Similarly, in Method Prayer, the practitioner approaches their spiritual journey with the same careful deliberation. Each prayer, each whispered word or heartfelt cry, serves as a testament to the soul's yearning. These aren't just words; they are hues of hope, shades of gratitude, and tints of supplication, all contributing to the masterpiece of one's spiritual narrative.

What differentiates Method Prayer from other spiritual exercises is its emphasis on conscious engagement. It is not about reciting learned verses or mindlessly repeating invocations. It's about engaging with each word, understanding its essence, and channelling its power to forge a connection with the divine. In this practice, intentionality is the force that drives the heart's compass towards its true north – the divine.

As practitioners delve deeper into this art form, a transformation unfolds. The bond with the divine strengthens, evolving from a distant echo to a resonant dialogue. The soul, once adrift in the vast ocean of spiritual exploration, now finds its anchor in the harbour of intentionality. With each prayer, the practitioner adds another layer to their spiritual tapestry, weaving patterns of hope, gratitude, and devotion.

However, this art form is not a solitary endeavour. The beauty of intentionality in Method Prayer lies in the collaborative dance between the individual and the divine. It recognizes that while we might set the stage with our intentions, it's the divine that breathes life into our aspirations, guiding our brushstrokes with grace and wisdom.

But why is intentionality so crucial in crafting this spiritual masterpiece? Because it instils a sense of agency and purpose in the practitioner. In a world where spiritual paths can often seem preordained or prescribed, intentionality carves out a space for personal exploration and discovery. It's a call to be an active participant in one's spiritual narrative, to take charge of one's journey, and to co-create a path that aligns with both heart and higher calling.

The art of intentionality in Method Prayer is a transformative practice that beckons individuals to approach their spiritual journey as master artists. With the canvas of the soul spread out before them, they are empowered to paint a vivid tapestry of their spiritual aspirations, guided by intentionality and infused with divine grace. As each brushstroke adds depth and dimension to their spiritual masterpiece, practitioners find themselves not just reciting prayers, but living them, crafting a luminous narrative that shines with the brilliance of divine communion.

The Palette of Emotions: Painting a Spiritual Journey

In the vast expanse of spiritual practices, Method Prayer stands as a unique intersection where emotions meet devotion. Within this practice, emotions aren't just transient feelings; they are akin to vibrant colours that illuminate the canvas of one's spiritual narrative. This isn't just a silent canvas waiting to be painted but a living tapestry where each emotion finds its space and resonance, enhancing the dialogue with the divine.

Picture a painter's palette, a treasure trove of hues, each one a testament to the myriad of human emotions. As practitioners of Method Prayer, we are akin to painters. Our canvas is the realm of spiritual discourse, and our colours are the diverse emotions we experience in our daily lives. With each dip into this emotional palette, we draw forth shades of joy, pools of sorrow, strokes of love, and dabs of awe. As the brush moves, it is not just painting; it is conversing, pouring out the heart's contents in a dance of colours and sentiments.

Joy, in this artistic process, isn't just a transient feeling; it's a vivid splash of yellow, illuminating the canvas with its brilliance. It becomes an effervescent expression, a testament to moments of happiness, gratitude, and the beauty of life. Each joyful brushstroke is a celebration, a reminder of the blessings and the cherished moments that make life meaningful.

Sorrow, often perceived as a sombre shade, adds depth and character to the spiritual canvas. It isn't a void but a deep blue, representing moments of reflection, healing, and growth. Through the veil of sorrow, we find ourselves seeking comfort and solace, and in this process, we draw closer to the divine, seeking answers and understanding.

Love, the most profound of emotions, is painted with a warm and enveloping red. It's more than just a feeling; it's an essence that binds us to the divine. With each stroke imbued with love, we forge an unbreakable bond, a thread of connection that intertwines our souls with the sacred. It's in this loving embrace that we find our prayers resonating with passion, devotion, and a deep sense of belonging.

Awe, a sublime shade of purple, graces the canvas with its majesty. It's an emotion that envelopes us, reminding us of the grandeur and wonder of the divine. Each dab of awe is a moment of realization, an acknowledgement of the vastness of the universe and the divine's magnificence.

In this transformative journey of Method Prayer, emotions transcend their typical definitions. They evolve into a vibrant language, an eloquent dialect that speaks of our deepest yearnings and experiences. This emotional dialogue, filled with the hues of joy, sorrow, love, and awe, becomes a resonant testament of our authentic self, a mirror reflecting our unique spiritual journey.

In conclusion, within Method Prayer, the palette of emotions serves as a bridge, connecting our human experiences with the divine realm. As we paint our spiritual narratives with these vivid colours, we craft a masterpiece that not only reflects our individuality but also our profound communion with the sacred. It's a journey where our heartbeats and emotions sync in harmony, creating a symphony that reverberates in the vast halls of the divine.

Integrating the Sacred: Infusing Divinity into Everyday Life

Method Prayer isn't just a ritual or a fixed practice meant only for particular sanctified spaces or celebratory occasions. Instead, it's a living philosophy, a way of life that threads through the very core of our existence, turning the most ordinary moments into avenues of deep, divine connection. By weaving the principles of Method Prayer into the daily tapestry of life, we frame our mundane actions within the golden borders of sacredness, inviting a richer understanding and appreciation of the world around us.

In today's fast-paced world, where time seems to slip through our fingers, and routines become monotonous, it's easy to overlook the magic in the mundane. We often go through our daily chores mechanically, hardly pausing to appreciate the intricacies of the world around us. However, the practice of Method Prayer challenges this status quo. It prompts us to stop, reflect, and find spiritual significance in our day-to-day tasks and experiences.

Consider the simple act of washing dishes. On the surface, it might seem like a chore – an activity to get done quickly. But through the lens of Method Prayer, it transforms into a ritual of mindfulness and reverence. As you touch the water, feel the smooth surface of the dishes, and watch the bubbles form from the soap, you are reminded of nature's wonders and the divine's blessings. The act becomes more than just cleaning; it's a moment of profound gratitude for the food that was on those dishes, the hands that prepared it, and the universe that provided the ingredients. The water isn't just a cleaning agent, but a symbol of life's flow, purifying and renewing. Thus, a simple household task evolves into a sacred ritual, full of depth and meaning.

Taking a stroll through your neighbourhood or local park offers another opportunity to practice Method Prayer. Every step can be a gentle reminder of our connection to the Earth and the divine energy that pulses through every living being. The rustling leaves tell stories of age-old wisdom, while the blossoming flowers speak of rebirth and hope. When we immerse ourselves in these moments, truly present and engaged, our walks become meditative journeys. They become our personal pilgrimage, where each step is a prayer, a silent expression of love and gratitude for the wonders of creation.

The daily commute, often riddled with impatience and monotony, too holds the potential for transformation. Instead of viewing it as a tedious necessity, Method Prayer allows us to turn these moments into sacred pauses. The journey can become a space for introspection, for setting intentions, or simply for acknowledging the divine presence that permeates everything. The sights and sounds during the commute, whether it's the hum of the engine or the fleeting landscapes, can serve as reminders of the vast, intricate world we are a part of. Method Prayer isn't about compartmentalizing the sacred and the mundane. It's about recognizing the inherent divinity in every moment, no matter how ordinary it may seem. By integrating this practice into daily life, we're not just enhancing our spiritual connection, but also enriching our overall life experience. We begin to see the world with fresh eyes, appreciating the myriad ways the divine communicates with us. This daily infusion of sacredness serves as a reminder that every moment holds the potential for connection, gratitude, and awe. Through Method Prayer, our lives become a beautiful mosaic, where even the tiniest fragments shine with divine light, painting a masterpiece of sacred significance.

Chapter 4
Method Prayer: The Spiritual Canvas of Divine Connection

In every stroke of an artist's brush lies a tale, a memory, a sentiment waiting to be shared with the world. Much like a canvas bears the soul of an artist, the heart carries the profound tales of our spiritual journeys. Nestled within these tales is the art of Method Prayer, an avenue that allows us to channel our innermost emotions, dreams, and aspirations, painting them with hues of faith and connection. Dive deeper with me into this spiritual art form, where each prayer, each chant, and each reflection become a brushstroke on the vast canvas of our souls.

The Palette of Method Prayer

The world of Method Prayer is reminiscent of an artist's toolbox – rich, diverse, and profound. Within it lie tools not of bristles or colours but of deep, resonant practices designed to bring out the very essence of our spiritual beings. These practices, whether they are the comforting cadences of a chant, the introspective musings penned in a journal, the tactile grounding of prayer beads, or the heart-warming notes of sacred hymns, act as our brushes, guiding our hands as we trace our spiritual paths.

As you navigate through this enriching world, you'll realize that each technique, each method is more than just a practice. They're individual expressions, unique brushstrokes that narrate our personal tales of faith, commitment, and divine communion. Our spiritual canvas, thus, becomes a mosaic of these myriad practices, each tile resonating with the echoes of our individual connections with the divine.

Sensory Awareness: The Preliminary Sketch

Before the colours meet the canvas, an artist sketches, laying down the foundational lines that guide the final masterpiece. Sensory awareness plays a similar role in Method Prayer. It forms the foundational sketch, guiding us as we fill our canvas with richer experiences. This practice revolves around the art of the present, of being so deeply engrossed in the current moment that every sensation, every sound, every scent paints a vivid image in our minds.

In our technologically driven era, where the digital realm often blurs the beauty of the present, sensory awareness emerges as a beacon. It calls upon us to disconnect from the virtual and reconnect with the real. It beckons us to listen – to the rustle of leaves, the babble of a brook, the melodies of morning birds. To feel – the warmth of the sun, the kiss of the wind, the pulse of life around us. And to see, not with just our eyes but with our hearts, recognizing the divine that dances in every dewdrop and sunset.

This practice isn't just about passive observation; it's an active celebration. A celebration of the world in its raw, unfiltered beauty. Every sensation we immerse ourselves in becomes a brushstroke, capturing moments of raw, unfiltered beauty. Through sensory awareness, we realize that the sacred doesn't solely reside in age-old scriptures or grand temples. It thrives in every corner of our existence, awaiting our acknowledgement.

Method Prayer is more than a series of practices. See it as your spiritual art studio, where every corner is filled with the tools you need to paint your unique journey. With each day, as you pick up these tools, you add another stroke, another shade, and another contour to your masterpiece.

Whether you are a seasoned spiritual traveller or a curious beginner, Method Prayer offers something for everyone. It encourages you to become the artist of your spiritual realm, to hold your brushes with confidence and to paint with passion. In this art form, there are no mistakes, only lessons. No strict guidelines, only free-flowing expressions. Your canvas, your rules.

And as your canvas fills with the colours of your experiences, reflections, and emotions, it becomes a testament – a testament to your unique journey, your individual relationship with the divine, and your ever-evolving spiritual narrative. Through Method Prayer, you're not just creating a work of art; you're crafting a legacy of faith, devotion, and divine connection—a legacy that will inspire many more spiritual artists to pick up their brushes and begin their own journeys.

Emotional Reflection: The Colours of the Heart in Method Prayer

A masterful painter, when faced with a blank canvas, doesn't merely apply paint without thought or feeling. Every colour chosen, and every brushstroke made, is a testament to the depth of emotion and experience that the artist wishes to convey. Similarly, Method Prayer offers an avenue for the spiritual seeker to explore the emotional depths within, turning feelings into a vibrant palette with which to communicate with the divine. The art of emotional reflection stands central in this process, making the act of prayer not just a ritual, but a heartfelt dialogue.

The Spectrum of Emotions in Prayer

Emotions are the very essence of our human experience. They colour our world, influence our decisions, and shape our interactions. Just as an artist wouldn't limit themselves to a single colour, one should not stifle the range of emotions when diving into Method Prayer. These emotions, from the euphoric highs of joy to the melancholic lows of sorrow, play an instrumental role in crafting a sincere and meaningful dialogue with the divine.

Joy: The Radiant Hues of Happiness

Picture a morning sun, casting its golden glow upon the world, filling every corner with light and warmth. This is the emotion of joy – bright, uplifting, and full of promise. In Method Prayer, joy becomes a beautiful yellow or radiant orange, splashed across the canvas of your heart. It's in those moments of gratitude, the instances of unexpected kindness, or the simple pleasures that life brings. When you tap into this emotion during your prayers, it creates a bond of positivity and appreciation with the divine, celebrating the blessings that abound.

Sorrow: The Deep Blues of Desolation

However, not all emotions are as luminous as joy. There are times when grief engulfs us, casting everything in shades of blue and purple. Sorrow is an essential part of the human experience. It's the ache of heartbreak, the void left by loss, or the weight of regrets. Method Prayer doesn't shy away from these emotions. Instead, it encourages embracing them, allowing the tears to become the paint, and the heart's heaviness the brushstroke. In sharing our grief with the divine, we find a comforting embrace, a silent acknowledgement that our pain is seen and felt.

Hope: The Green Sprouts of Anticipation

Amidst the varied colours of emotions, hope stands out as a fresh green, reminiscent of new shoots sprouting from the earth. It's the twinkle in the eyes looking towards the future, the whispered prayers for better days, and the faith that good will always follow the bad. In Method Prayer, hope is celebrated and amplified. It's the anchor that grounds us, ensuring that even in our darkest moments, we have a tether to hold onto, connecting us to the divine and the promises of tomorrow.

Fear: The Shadows That Seek Light

Fear, with its dark greys and ominous blacks, often casts shadows across our hearts. It's the nagging doubt, the looming uncertainty, and the apprehension of what lies ahead. Yet, even in its darkness, Method Prayer offers a beacon. By acknowledging and sharing our fears in this sacred space, we allow them to be illuminated, seeking guidance and solace from a higher power. This cathartic release, much like an artist using contrast in a painting, adds depth and perspective to our spiritual journey.

Emotions as the Bridge to Authentic Connection

Emotional reflection in Method Prayer isn't just about identifying feelings; it's about harnessing them as a bridge to the divine. When emotions become the medium, prayers transform from rehearsed words to authentic conversations. They reveal the raw, unfiltered essence of our beings, making every plea, gratitude, or reflection a genuine expression of our soul's state.

Just as an artist creates a masterpiece by blending various colours, a practitioner of Method Prayer crafts a unique spiritual journey by embracing the full spectrum of emotions. The canvas of the heart, when painted with genuine feelings, becomes a testament to the true nature of one's relationship with the divine. Through the art of emotional reflection, Method Prayer becomes a deeply personal, enriching, and transformative experience, resonating with the true colours of the heart.

Deepening Your Spiritual Journey: Engaging with the Sacred Texts

In the realm of spiritual practices, scriptural meditation stands out as a profound method of connecting with the divine. It is akin to an artist studying the works of the masters, seeking inspiration and guidance. This method allows practitioners to delve into the depths of ancient wisdom and embrace the teachings of the sacred texts, enriching their spiritual journey and deepening their understanding of the divine.

Imagine a budding artist standing before a masterpiece painted by a great artist from a bygone era. They examine every brushstroke, every shade, and every nuance, seeking to understand the essence of what the artist intended to convey. In the same vein, in scriptural meditation, the seeker immerses themselves in the scriptures, pondering each word, phrase, and teaching, striving to grasp the profound wisdom encapsulated within.

The scriptures, like timeless art pieces, have layers of meaning that unfold as one contemplates them. On the surface, they may offer moral teachings, historical narratives, or prophetic visions. Yet, as one delves deeper, they reveal intricate patterns of spiritual truths, insights about the nature of the divine, and the mysteries of the universe. Just as an artist gazes upon a painting to derive inspiration, a seeker immerses themselves in the scriptures to derive spiritual guidance.

Engaging with the scriptures is not a mere intellectual exercise. It is a heart-centred endeavour, where the seeker approaches the texts with reverence, humility, and an open heart. This approach allows them to resonate with the divine wisdom embedded within, facilitating a transformative experience. As an artist draws inspiration from a masterpiece, the seeker draws spiritual nourishment from the scriptures, feeding their soul and bolstering their spiritual journey.

One of the foundational aspects of scriptural meditation is contemplative reading. This method involves slowly and deliberately reading a passage, reflecting on its meaning, and allowing its essence to permeate the consciousness. Just as an artist might study a painting in detail, noting its composition, colour schemes, and techniques, the seeker ponders the scriptures, absorbing their profound teachings and integrating them into their spiritual practice.

Incorporating scriptural meditation into daily life has profound benefits. It serves as a constant reminder of the divine presence, guiding the seeker in their daily endeavours and decisions. Just as an artist carries the influence of the masters in their work, the seeker carries the wisdom of the scriptures in their heart, allowing it to shape their thoughts, actions, and interactions.

Furthermore, the practice fosters a deep sense of connection with the divine. As the seeker engages with the scriptures, they establish a dialogue with the divine, much like an artist communicates with their muse. This dialogue is a sacred exchange, where the seeker receives guidance, inspiration, and insights, enriching their spiritual journey.

The scriptures, like masterpieces, are timeless. They have spoken to countless souls across ages, offering solace, guidance, and enlightenment. In today's fast-paced world, scriptural meditation provides a sanctuary, a space where the seeker can retreat, reconnect with the divine, and rejuvenate their spirit. Just as an artist finds solace in the classics, the seeker finds peace in the scriptures, drawing strength and inspiration for their spiritual journey.

Scriptural meditation is a profound practice that deepens the seeker's connection with the divine, enriching their spiritual journey. Just as an artist studies the classics to refine their craft, the seeker engages with the scriptures to hone their spiritual understanding. By immersing themselves in the ancient wisdom of the sacred texts, they draw inspiration, guidance, and strength, painting a vibrant canvas of their spiritual journey, filled with the hues of divine wisdom and grace.

Active Dialogue with God: An Artist's Spiritual Conversation

Method Prayer is a profound spiritual journey where one's soul engages in a deep dialogue with the divine. This interaction mirrors the intimate conversation an artist has with their muse while painting. The essence of this chapter is to elucidate the sacred art of this active dialogue, emphasizing how, like an artist connecting with their muse, one can attune to the divine's presence, responding to its guidance and the wisdom arising from the soul's depths.

Visualize an artist poised in front of a blank canvas, ready to translate the essence of their muse onto this space. Similarly, in Method Prayer, our hearts and souls serve as the canvas, and the divine presence is the muse we wish to portray.

When practising Method Prayer, our prayers evolve into more than just a recitation of words. They become a living dialogue – a pulsating exchange akin to a harmonious dance between words and silence. The seeker, in this instance, is both a speaker and an attentive listener. This dialogue signifies that the divine is not a distant entity but an ever-present guide in our spiritual odyssey.

Just as an artist deeply observes every subtle detail of their muse, you too, during this prayer, develop a heightened sensitivity to the gentle nudges and signs from the divine. This profound connection isn't merely a language-bound interaction. It goes beyond words and logic, tapping into the soul's profound depths. It's about being in sync with the divine, cultivating openness, receptivity, and active engagement in this spiritual dialogue.

The beauty of this active dialogue is that it isn't restricted to designated prayer times or ritualistic settings. It seamlessly integrates into daily life, similar to how an artist is constantly inspired by their muse. Every life scenario, be it moments of solitude in your room, peaceful nature experiences, or the daily urban hustle, offers an opportunity to commune with the divine.

Engaging in this dialogue, you'll realize the divine isn't just a spectator but an intimate partner in your spiritual progression. Analogous to an artist discovering varied shades of their muse with each brushstroke, you too delve deeper into the divine's essence with each prayer. These prayers become exploratory tools, pathways to fathom and bond with the divine on a deeply personal level.

This dialogue's wisdom doesn't exclusively descend from a higher power. Instead, it emanates from within, symbolizing a fusion of your distinct perspective and the boundless wisdom of the divine. Imagine an artist mixing colours on a palette to craft a unique shade. Similarly, your insights blend with divine guidance, resulting in revelations that are both personal and universally divine.

Silence, in this dialogue, is as powerful as spoken words. An artist values the canvas's negative space as much as their vibrant brush strokes. In the same vein, during moments of silence and stillness, one can deeply sense the divine's presence. It's during these quiet moments that the soul's profoundest connections are established, and the most enlightening insights are gained.

As one delves deeper into Method Prayer, it becomes evident that this divine dialogue isn't bound by temporal or spatial constraints. It surpasses the mundane, transforming every instant into a significant rendezvous with the divine. Just as an artist's conversation with their muse imparts life to a painting, your dialogue with the divine infuses your spiritual journey with richness, depth, and transformational energy. This spiritual dialogue not only resonates with the soul but also shapes the very core of our being, crafting a magnificent tableau of communion that's both sanctified and awe-inspiring.

The Canvas of Life: Brushstrokes of Spirit-Led Action

Within the intricate tapestry of our lives lies the potential for an extraordinary masterpiece, a living portrait imbued with the vibrancy of divine guidance. This is particularly apparent in the practice of Method Prayer, which transcends mere rituals and shapes the entirety of our existence. Like a seasoned artist, every spiritually inclined individual holds the potential to craft a life teeming with purpose, intention, and divinely inspired actions.

Every artist understands that a canvas, while seemingly passive and unassuming, holds infinite possibilities. Similarly, our lives, no matter how ordinary they may seem, can be transformed into a rich tapestry of experiences, all guided by the whispers of the divine. This guidance, termed 'spirit-led action', serves as the guiding hand that shapes and moulds our daily actions, interactions, and decisions.

As you envision your life as this expansive canvas, consider the role of spirit-led action as the brushstrokes that define and enhance its beauty. These are not mere impulsive gestures, but intentional actions inspired by divine nudges. They could manifest in a variety of ways – perhaps as an unexpected act of kindness, a moment of patience during adversity, or a decision to embark on a new journey resonating with one's spiritual calling.

An artist knows the importance of each colour on their palette, selecting each hue with deliberate care to evoke specific sentiments and emotions. In the same vein, spirit-led actions guide individuals to colour their deeds with love, sincerity, and authenticity. Every choice, every gesture, becomes an embodiment of one's deep-seated connection to a higher power.

Yet, the journey of crafting this masterpiece isn't devoid of challenges. Just as an artist grapple with the intricacies of their medium, individuals often confront obstacles that test their faith and resilience. However, it is in the heart of these challenges that the true essence of spirit-led action emerges. Every hurdle is seen not as a hindrance but as an invitation to grow, to evolve, and to paint one's canvas with even richer, deeper hues of experience and understanding.

Moreover, this divinely guided journey is not an isolated endeavour. As each brushstroke contributes to the broader image, every spirit-led action ripples outward, influencing the world in ways both seen and unseen. Thus, one's spiritual journey becomes intertwined with the collective journey of humanity, creating a shared narrative of love, growth, and connection.

Life, when approached with this perspective, evolves into an ever-unfolding artwork. Each day becomes an opportunity to dip one's brush into the palette of divine wisdom, creating patterns and motifs that speak of a higher purpose. The practice of spirit-led action anchors individuals in the present, allowing them to move through each moment with awareness, intention, and a deep reverence for the divine dance of existence.

In essence, the canvas of life, when painted with the brushstrokes of spirit-led action, becomes a testament to the transformative power of divine alignment. It stands as a reminder that every individual holds the potential to craft a life that is not just lived, but exquisitely and purposefully painted. Through this alignment, each person can craft a life that resonates with the melodies of the divine, a masterpiece that, in its entirety, sings of love, purpose, and profound spiritual connection.

Conclusion

The realm of spirituality is akin to an artist's studio, wherein every practitioner possesses a blank canvas waiting to be imbued with the strokes of experience, introspection, and Divine connection. At the forefront of this artistic endeavour is Method Prayer, a practice that beckons every soul to craft their own spiritual masterpiece. It's an art that extends beyond religious rituals, guiding the artist – each one of us – in the intricate dance of life and spirituality.

As we delve deeper into the essence of Method Prayer, it's vital to visualize oneself in the quiet sanctuary of a studio, surrounded by the tools of the craft. The canvas represents your life, untouched and waiting for the first brushstroke. This brushstroke, inspired by the rhythms of Method Prayer, sets the tone for the entire masterpiece.

Each prayer, meditation, and moment of introspection adds depth and texture to the canvas. The beauty lies not in perfection but in the authenticity of each stroke, the raw emotion conveyed, and the connection to the Divine. The relationship with the Almighty isn't just a solitary note but a harmonious symphony that enriches the entirety of your existence.

Method Prayer is not a rigid set of guidelines to be followed, but rather a fluid framework allowing personal interpretation. As an artist is free to experiment with different techniques and mediums, so are you encouraged to explore the depths of your connection with the Divine. There's a profound freedom in knowing that there isn't a "right" or "wrong" way, but merely an expression of your spiritual essence.

Challenges and moments of doubt may arise, much like an artist might question a specific choice or direction in their artwork. However, these moments are not setbacks but opportunities. They add layers of complexity to the canvas, making the final masterpiece richer and more profound. Through Method Prayer, you learn to navigate these challenges, understanding that every obstacle refines your spiritual journey, much like the meticulous detailing of a painting.

The beauty of this spiritual artwork is that it's never truly complete. With each day, new experiences, insights, and revelations add to the canvas. This ongoing nature of the masterpiece signifies the eternal evolution of one's spiritual journey. Just as great artists leave certain works unfinished, allowing for continual interpretation and growth, your spiritual narrative is forever evolving, with Method Prayer as the guiding hand.

Moreover, Method Prayer teaches us that the canvas of spirituality is not an individual endeavour. While it's a deeply personal journey, it also intertwines with the world around us. Each prayer, reflection, and act of kindness adds vibrancy to not only our own spiritual canvas but also the collective tapestry of humanity.

In conclusion, the journey of Method Prayer is an invitation to embrace the artist within and to recognize the canvas of life as a platform for spiritual expression and connection. It's a call to immerse oneself in the art of divine conversation, to let the soul's desires and aspirations flow freely, crafting a masterpiece that resonates with authenticity and Divine connection.

This exploration of Method Prayer is not an end but a beautiful beginning. It's the dawn of a journey that promises growth, transformation, and an ever-deepening bond with the Divine. In the spirit of eternal exploration, let us continue to wield the brush of spirituality, painting our masterpiece with the colours of love, faith, and divine grace, and may the artistry of Method Prayer illuminate our path, guiding us towards the eternal embrace of the Divine.